# THINGS THAT SHINE: POEMS

## ARIANE SIGNER

BALBOA
PRESS
A DIVISION OF HAY HOUSE

Copyright © 2019 Ariane Signer.

Interior Graphics/Art Credit: Ella Brown

All rights reserved. No part of this book may be used or reproduced by any means, graphic, electronic, or mechanical, including photocopying, recording, taping or by any information storage retrieval system without the written permission of the author except in the case of brief quotations embodied in critical articles and reviews.

Balboa Press books may be ordered through booksellers or by contacting:

Balboa Press
A Division of Hay House
1663 Liberty Drive
Bloomington, IN 47403
www.balboapress.com
1 (877) 407-4847

Because of the dynamic nature of the Internet, any web addresses or links contained in this book may have changed since publication and may no longer be valid. The views expressed in this work are solely those of the author and do not necessarily reflect the views of the publisher, and the publisher hereby disclaims any responsibility for them.

The author of this book does not dispense medical advice or prescribe the use of any technique as a form of treatment for physical, emotional, or medical problems without the advice of a physician, either directly or indirectly. The intent of the author is only to offer information of a general nature to help you in your quest for emotional and spiritual well-being. In the event you use any of the information in this book for yourself, which is your constitutional right, the author and the publisher assume no responsibility for your actions.

Any people depicted in stock imagery provided by Getty Images are models, and such images are being used for illustrative purposes only. Certain stock imagery © Getty Images.

Print information available on the last page.

ISBN: 978-1-9822-2150-8 (sc)
ISBN: 978-1-9822-2151-5 (e)

Balboa Press rev. date: 02/12/2019

For Thomas, Theo & Jake
You are the brightest stars I have ever seen.

"Perhaps all the dragons in our lives are princesses who are only waiting to see us act, just once, with beauty and courage. Perhaps everything that frightens us is, in its deepest essence, something helpless that wants our love."
— Rainer Maria Rilke, <u>Letters to a Young Poet</u>

# Acknowledgements

This collection would have never seen the light of day without the continuous support of my husband, Thomas. Thank you for believing in my dreams and doing everything possible to help them come true. We make pretty magical things happen together, don't we? I will never stop loving you.

To my two son-shines, Theo and Jake. You have inspired me in ways that I could never have imagined. Thank you for showing up when you did. You have given me the most beautiful love that I have ever known.

Mom and Dad, I'm eternally grateful that I was born into a family that appreciated books. Thank you for never turning down my Scholastic book order requests, for reading my short stories, and for believing in the power of my imagination.

And Mom, you especially, have been my creative inspiration for as long as I can remember. Your storytelling is more than just the recounting of tales. It's pure magic. Thank you for always being my safe place, where I could share my thoughts and feelings, without judgement. You are a beautiful and artistic soul, and your support has been an essential part of my journey.

Veronica, for all the talks, advice and long-distance support, I thank you. Living far away from you is rough and tough, but I am so proud of how we have shown up for each other emotionally and spiritually over the last 3 years! You are such a blessing in my life. I love you.

To Ruth, Mike and Alexis. Thank you for welcoming me so lovingly into your family. I really lucked out to have such amazing in-laws. I am forever grateful for everything you have done for our little family. Je vous aimes.

To my step-family in England, I love you all, thank you for being such fun, colourful characters. Julie, I never imagined that one day I would swap surnames with my stepmother! Our family history is stranger than fiction, but never boring, right?!

To my core Canadian trio, Ashley, Stef and Erica. Thank you for coming to Switzerland and swimming in the Timberlaken with me! Thank you for supporting and loving me, always. Nothing feels better than friends that have known you since you accidentally caught on fire in high school.

To my dear friends Nicolas, Seona, Natasha, Kristen, Michelle. I miss you, and I love you. Thank you for enjoying my often-exaggerated retelling of life events.

To Sally, for seeing the sparkle in me, even when I couldn't see it, myself. What a miraculous meeting we had, right? Perfect timing, babe. You are a true and beautiful soul, and I am grateful for your support, coaching and friendship. You will change the world with your work!

To Shawna, for being my soul sister from the beginning. You have supported my spiritual life for close to two decades, and our chats have always eased my anxieties and made me feel like a living, breathing miracle (I can picture you reading this and screaming, *YOU ARE!*) For the countless tarot card readings, hypnosis sessions, crystals, sleepovers and supportive emails, thank you.

To Svetlana, for believing in me, both professionally and personally. You touched my heart in a very special way, even with your severe Eastern European ways (smile). I miss our little chats.

To Vikki, for being a great friend during a period of so much change in my life. I'm grateful that we found each other.

Special thanks to Ella Brown for capturing my creative vision beautifully during our photo shoot in Lenzburg, Switzerland.

To my team at Balboa Press, Virginia Morrel, May Emerson and Taylor Kopplin, thank you for your guidance and support during this very new, and very exciting experience.

And finally, to all the past and future versions of myself, I love you. Feel the fear, and do it anyway, girl.

<3

# Introduction

Having two babies under the age of two has affected my attention span, so I have no choice but to write out this introduction in bullet form:

1. Hi! Thank you so much for picking up a copy of my book. I really hope you enjoy it.
2. I never meant to write a collection of poems. In fact, I hadn't written a poem in over twenty years, before starting this collection.
3. I was writing an autobiographical memoir about my journey to sobriety, when this collection got underway. Struck with a pretty severe case of writer's block, I did what I normally do when life goes to shit. I asked the Universe for divine intervention/a sign/ a dream/ a symbol of what to do next. Believe it or not, I woke up that night and wrote the poem *John* on my phone. No idea why I was thinking of Cuban John in the middle of the night, but I'm grateful for the Universe's involvement (and sense of humour)!
4. Side note: this happened on 11/11/2018, which was allegedly the most powerful manifesting date of the decade. I am a believer!
5. You might have guessed by now that I am really into the following things. The Universe. Asking the Universe for help and guidance. Signs. Symbols. Numbers. Numerical symmetry. Coincidences. Synchronicities. Magic. The moon. Eclipses. The sun. Planets in general. Space. Time. Writing about signs, symbols, synchronicities....
6. The entire collection was written in three months. I wrote A LOT OF POEMS. Not all of them made the cut for publication. Very few of the poems in this collection are in their original format. I did a lot of editing (re: doubting myself) before sending to print.

7. The poems are sorted into two sections, The Shadow and The Shimmer. This reference is a nod to my blog, established in early 2016, called *The Shadow* and *The Shimmer*. You can visit that here: www.theshadowandtheshimmer.blogspot.com
8. The Shadow section deals with the darker, more challenging and painful moments in my life.
9. The Shimmer deals with the more optimistic, happy and joyous moments in my life.
10. My feelings, emotions and experiences make me a complete human. I didn't accept this for many years. I am far less judgmental of my emotional and mental states, these days. Writing and sharing these poems has been very therapeutic for me; if I can make one or two people feel a little less alone, I will consider this a win (it's already a win, though. Writing a book has been on my bucket list for over a decade. If you're slow and steady, put your hands up!).
11. Each section has 44 poems, because I'm obsessed with the number 44. I also like 22, 11, 13, 7......
12. I can't leave this at 12 points, because it's not one of my magical numbers.
13. Ah. That's better. Happy reading!

Ariane

# Contents

## The Shadow

| | |
|---|---|
| 1 | THE BACKWARDS JOURNEY |
| 3 | FEAR DRAGON |
| 5 | DADDY ISSUES I |
| 7 | YOUR SISTER |
| 9 | CODEPENDENCY |
| 11 | ACCIDENT PRONE |
| 13 | BREAK-UPS |
| 15 | INDIA |
| 17 | OVERALL |
| 19 | BEFORE THE TROUBLE BEGAN |
| 21 | DUMPSTER JUICE |
| 23 | BEING SET FREE |
| 25 | JOHN |
| 27 | OVERSIZED SHIRTS |
| 29 | LOW LOW |
| 31 | DEMONS |
| 33 | RUN FOR THE HILLS |
| 35 | THRILLING |
| 37 | HOW HOT |
| 39 | DRUNKEN ARRANGEMENTS |
| 41 | MY TYPE |
| 43 | THE LAST ONE ON EARTH |
| 45 | BODY ISSUES |
| 47 | TRANSFORM |
| 49 | TRACKING |
| 51 | A BIT BORING |
| 53 | TRAINS |

| | |
|---|---|
| 55 | THE FIRST NIGHT |
| 57 | GHOSTS |
| 59 | OLIVE BRANCHES |
| 61 | WE KNOW |
| 63 | THE CLIMB |
| 65 | THE FOG |
| 67 | DARK PLACES |
| 69 | HOT TUB PARTIES |
| 71 | SMALL TOWNS |
| 73 | PLANES |
| 75 | DISAPPEARING PEOPLE |
| 77 | MOM BRAIN |
| 79 | GHOSTS PART II |
| 81 | BROWN EYES |
| 83 | EXHAUSTION |
| 85 | ELEPHANT IN THE ROOM |
| 87 | THE TRUTH |

## The Shimmer

| | |
|---|---|
| 93 | PRUD'HOMME |
| 95 | ON THE FENCE |
| 97 | MIAMI AIRPORT |
| 99 | YOUR DARKNESS |
| 101 | JUST ARIANE |
| 103 | AT FIRST |
| 105 | JUNE 15, 2015 |
| 107 | PARIS |
| 109 | SHEEPS |
| 111 | TONY ROBBINS |
| 113 | TIRUPUR |
| 115 | SCARY BITS |

| | |
|---|---|
| 117 | KAREN JONES' DAUGHTER |
| 119 | PROPOSAL |
| 121 | THINGS THAT SHINE |
| 123 | SWITZERLAND, 2014 |
| 125 | ROOFTOPS |
| 127 | NO SURRENDER |
| 129 | BABY BOY |
| 131 | PARADOX |
| 133 | LABELS |
| 135 | REINVENT |
| 137 | ON IMMIGRATING TO A NEW COUNTRY |
| 139 | SPAS |
| 141 | BAJAN SUN |
| 143 | PLANETS NEAR PLUTO |
| 145 | LITTLE PARTICLES |
| 147 | FALCON |
| 149 | JUST A MIST |
| 151 | PINK CLOUDS |
| 153 | IN THE VALLEY |
| 155 | BLOOD MOON ECLIPSE |
| 157 | SVETLANA |
| 159 | 11 22 |
| 161 | NEVER RETRACT |
| 163 | THREE SANDWICHES |
| 165 | THE WORDS |
| 167 | I GAVE UP |
| 169 | SWEET AND STRONG |
| 171 | FRESHLY CUT GRASS |
| 173 | SHINING BEAUTIFULLY |
| 175 | THE BRIGHT SIDE |
| 177 | LEARNING HOW TO BE ALIVE |
| 179 | A FINAL THOUGHT |

# The Shadow

# The Backwards Journey

This part may be emotional and difficult-
the backwards journey-
but in going back-
I can finally nurture, love and protect
those vulnerable sides of me
that really need to be put back together.

# Fear Dragon

Here I am pushing away that beautiful beautifulness and bringing the dirty fear dragon into the mix.

## Daddy Issues I

demanding his love greedily,
fearing abandon in the most ridiculous ways-
essentially- pushing him away.
and this was the moment.
he thought we should break it off.
I cried and refused to accept it.
I begged him to take care of me and not leave.
finally, he agreed- probably too exhausted to continue the discussion.
he was basically a prisoner of love.

# Your Sister

Your sister died and I sent you a letter
With pink handwritten condolences
How could so much pain exist in a person
That I had kissed and met in parks
You had a lot of empty bottles and made
Beautiful music
I thought, perhaps, that helped
I wanted to be a part of what healed you
An impossible task, for a girl of fifteen
You were nice to me when we were alone,
But told the others I was just a vixen.
But still, I knew you saw me.
Your sister died, so I let you off easy.

# Codependency

unavailability only made me want him more.
imagining that he was doing something horrible.
He made it clear that he was not looking for a crazy girlfriend.
One day we got into a fight.
I was so upset that I drank an entire bottle of sparkling white wine in the bathtub,
crying uncontrollably.
When we were fighting, I couldn't concentrate on anything.
I obsessively wondered what he was thinking.
In my imagination, it was always the worst-case scenario.
He thinks I'm crazy and he's going to leave me.
I'm unlovable.
I'm not good enough.
He will notice eventually.

# Accident Prone

At the clinic, I was assessed
and it was confirmed that I would require 3 stitches in my upper lip,
a cast for the hairline fracture in my left wrist,
and I almost certainly had a mild concussion from the fall.
On top of this, I had cuts and bruises all over my knees and legs.
Looking down, I realized that I had soaked blood into
The oversized T-Shirt, that I took from your room.

# Break-ups

I broke up with him in a very inconsiderate way-
just sent him a text saying we had to talk-
and when he pushed me for details,
I told him it was over.
Months of horrible fights ensued.
The after-fights persisted for longer
Than the entire duration of our relationship.
We should've listened when they told us it was a terrible idea.

# India

how much exhaustion, heat, claustrophobia and fear can I take?
It's like going into the belly of the beast.
I want to go home with more courage

# Overall

Yes, he had a temper that sometimes showed itself-like that one night he threw a skateboard at me.
But overall, he was kind and respectful

# Before The Trouble Began

Before the trouble began we carved our names into wood at the Pelican Bar
In the Caribbean Sea, not far from Black River
Before the trouble began we made it to the top of the third highest volcano in the world,
Teide, and ate Spanish soup above the clouds
Before the trouble began, we skated on Lake Mildred in Jasper
I got distracted looking at elk and tripped on cracked ice
Before the trouble began we rode horses owned by Michael Douglas
In Mont-Tremblant; afterwards, a cozy fire and a pact to stay off of horses
Before the trouble began, we wrote each other emails, with detailed commentary
About what happened on that week's episode of *Survivor*
Before the trouble began, you let me paint the walls
Purple and mint and raspberry; the table turquoise
Before the trouble began we picked apples and kissed horses and built fires and sang "*When It Comes*" on long drives
Before the trouble began we swam at night in the North Atlantic Ocean
Somewhere off of Playa de las Americas, after too many glasses of wine
Before the trouble began we ziplined over YS Falls in Jamaica, and then did a professional waterfall photoshoot
I always planned elaborate activities, didn't I?
Before the trouble began we kissed in castles, and slept in boats and swam in cenotes, talking.
Before the trouble began we piled up boxes of treasures that we would take
into the future with us.
Before the trouble began we swore trouble would never come.

# DUMPSTER JUICE

When I went back to get my bike to go home-
I realized that my helmet was missing.
The boys were still around –
they told me that my helmet was in the dumpster.
They had removed all its' pads-
they were soaked in dumpster juice and impossible to retrieve.
I felt embarrassed and unworthy.
I thought that they liked me, but it was
A sabotage planned from the beginning.

# BEING SET FREE

All these changes in my life that
I'm so excited about
but sometimes I feel like I'm really alone.
Maybe I need to go through these feelings to come out
on the other side....
After how many years of hiding away from
everything with drinking-
maybe these things (tears) are surfacing and
finally escaping and being set free.

# John

I had a Cuban lover, once
He entered my life with impeccable timing
I needed him to help me get over another lover, who was more than just a lover, but that's another story.
He referred to his wife as his ex-wife, although she was not yet ex'ed
A small detail he forgot to mention.
That he was living with her still.
She sent me a message once to see if he was going home for dinner.
She seemed to have no issues with her not yet ex'ed husband having a lover, who, entirely by coincidence, shared a surname with her.
He used to pour rum into the corner of my kitchen as an offering to the spirits.
He mumbled a little something in Spanish each time.
I thought it was a neat ceremony, but a royal waste of booze.
It also activated my desire to mop the floors.
No one ever looked at me as intensely as he did.
He used to call me 'mamma'
It was the summer of 2011.
Our affair lasted about 30 days

# OVERSIZED SHIRTS

We biked off down the gravel path but they had gotten up to chase us.

I'm sure they had no intentions of actually hurting or raping us- but we didn't know that at the time.

As I biked faster and faster away, I turned to see if they were still close on my trail.

When I did this, I lost control of my bike and flew to the ground.

I slid on the mixture of gravel and broken glass and felt my face and knees scrape the ground.

When I realized what had happened,
the pain washing over me,
I looked down to my t-shirt (I still remember- it was one of dad's oversized shirts)
to see that it had turned from grey to bright red-
I was absolutely soaked in blood.

## Low Low

Some moments in life
Are inevitably lower than others
I can remember a low low
It involved sleeping on a children's mattress
On the floor of my new apartment
With the bed frame against the wall
Disassembled
And candles burning
Because
The lights weren't installed yet
I felt like my pain deserved such a medieval setting
Which also included
A large garbage bag over
The window
That looked out onto a sad street corner
And needed to be covered because I was on the first floor
Waking up to a stranger peering in
Would likely sink me further into despair
As if that was even possible
I sobbed until you left
It was nice of you to
Rent a moving truck
And set me up
After I told your family
All of your secrets
And ruined that year's Christmas

# DEMONS

A pretty face
But a broken spirit
They say time heals
But it's been years and
There are times when
I feel shattered
Bruises healed but
Heart's still battered
Make-up couldn't cover
The marks that you left
Under
With teeth and nails and
fists
Don't animals behave like this?
So much shame talking to
My mother
Afraid she would uncover
Little white lies
We told
This twisted game
Is getting old
Drink some more and
You'll forget it
Not conscious enough to
Even regret it
Just a blackout drunk who
Doesn't recall
Those nightmare nights
I remember them all
Eyes rolling back
Skidding off the tracks
Proof that the bottle
Can be worse

Than a heart attack
Can't run from your
Demons, they're quicker
And they don't disappear
If you drown them in liquor

# Run For The Hills

Your anger comes
With
Heavy steps and
Puffed breath;
Dragon in the flesh
Inability to cope
With feelings
Every comment
Has you reeling
Defensive and protective
Searching for fights
Like a detective
A child who never understood
How to channel
His bad moods
But you've brought this
Shit into
Adulthood
It's leaving me feeling
Like I should be
running for the hills
Where's it's safe
Wouldn't be my first time
Up that way
Its not my cross to
Bear
And your love's not worth
The fare
It the price is slow decay
My heart and soul
Withering away

# THRILLING

Strangely enough, she and I also had a violent side.
We would go outside at lunch-
stand near the main doors of the building
and take turns kicking each other's legs as hard as we could.
It was almost a competition of who could hurt the other person more.
I don't know why I engaged in this —
she was my very close friend —
but something about this game was thrilling.

# HOW HOT

Sigh.
You know how hot it would be if you
told me you were staying in to watch foreign films
and do vacation research and
write down your weird feelings that no one gets?!

# Drunken Arrangements

We drunkenly made an arrangement
to meet in the same basement the next weekend
I waited for you, by the piano.
With wine coloured lips and lingerie.
You decided it was safer to stay away.
You were a far better lover in my imagination, anyway.

# My Type

He was 35, kind of awkward/ugly but in a sort of cute way.
Older, weird.
But hey, for some reason it worked for me.
When we did finally get together for a drink,
I wasn't that impressed with his personality-
but I knew he was the type that I could escape with.

# The Last One On Earth

Wishing for someone
Who gets it
The way that I feel
The fears and
The magic
Someone who can
Inspire
Light a match
Set my soul on fire
Show me I'm not
The last one
On Earth to feel
So undone
Let me dream with you
Protected
From all the conflict
That's affected
My life, it's been infected
But also, so many
Blessings
Just have to do some
Weeding
Get rid of what's rotten
And plant some
New seedlings

# Body Issues

In Grade 3, after a summer of too many high-fat meals and TV time, I went back to school as a chubbier version of myself.
This would be the start of my body issues.
I was uncomfortable being bigger and sloppier than the rest of the fit and trim kids.
I felt ashamed- like my fat was a sign of weakness and lack of self-control.
Many days, I took my lunch into the bathroom and ate in a stall.
Some days, I threw out my lunch entirely, so I could sit with the kids at the lunch table and not feel embarrassed.
I was always ashamed of my "ugly" brown bread ham sandwiches- when all the kids had fun, hip lunches.
Sometimes I would accept snack handouts from their lunch bags.
When I ordered food from the cafeteria, I felt more "in" and "cool".
This was not usually a problem for me to sit and eat with friends – so long as the food was what everyone was eating.

# Transform

I want to transform my fear into
Something meaningful.
A story, or a song or a painting
Of a girl
Who lived many lives misunderstood
And walked with heavy steps
Through the neighbourhoods
Who looked at birds with envy
That they could fly from place to place
Without leaving shadows.
Who was always in awe of the wind
That held on to no pain
Blowing through space and time
Without a reason or a rhyme
Who wondered if others ever wondered as much as she did
About patterns and meaning and
Words whispered in the dark.
About fate and choice and the
Spaces in between.
And rode buses and trains, thinking of
All of the places she had and hadn't yet been.

# Tracking

Sometimes I get really tired of
Tracking things, numerically
After all, does it really matter that
I weighed 128 pounds at my lowest?
And walked 9 kilometres yesterday?
And swam 22 laps the day before?
Because my son was born on April 22, and I've always
Considered that number quite lucky, since
Will I ever look back and wonder why my heart rate was a low of
56 beats per minute in late October,
Or that at peak levels of exercise I kept it closer to 143 beats
Or that I like to eat cookies in two's, and if you take one from me,
I'll get another one to make it an even number again
I like numerical symmetry, but sometimes
I wonder why
I put so much energy into counting things that
One day, won't matter at all.

# A Bit Boring

He would get mad if I put something away where it "wasn't supposed to go".
I would get annoyed that all he did was watch TV and smoke weed.
We didn't do very many couple activities.
He didn't have a circle of friends, other than his cousin's gang in Toronto.
They weren't even that cool- so it was a bit boring.

# Trains

I drank on train tracks.
Nestled at the edge of our hometown
Teenagers gathered around
Drinking beers until we fell down
Setting fires and spilling secrets
Bonding over our families' regrets
Mosquitoes and cigarettes.
I cried on trains.
Lost in transit
Tears on the side of my designer
Jacket
No amount of high fashion can
Distract from it.
He doesn't really want you, girl
But you have made him your whole world
Just to escape the past turmoil.
I drank, waiting for trains.
He's far away, it's unfair.
One more cider and you won't care.
The sun's setting here,
But rising there.

# The First Night

The first night, I went home with him-
we drank a ton-
I took a cab home with my bra in my purse-
the world spinning from having indulged in way too much booze.

# Ghosts

We walked in the rain and
Talked about ghosts and how
Some overly sensitive people
Might be predisposed to feeling
The presence of spirits
And we agreed that we liked
Spirituality, but the thought of
Past lives made us nervous
For several reasons, but mainly
Because we didn't want to be responsible
If a past occupant of our soul
Had majorly messed up and
Had a karmic debt to pay
And I told you how
One girl, last year
Told me she saw a ghost
Perched upon my shoulder
It brought tears to her eyes
And to say the very least,
It made me feel unsettled
I was just there for our
Kids to play
Why overcomplicate everything?
And later that night, I cried
When I told my husband
Who understood that I was pregnant,
And maybe a little bit too sensitive
But then, several months later
An Indian man in town told me
That he saw a shadow surrounding
My aura
And I thought, well here
We go again dammit!

I might as well just hold up
A sign saying that I'm haunted
I'm still a lover of spiritual shit
But ghosts make me nervous
So leave them out of it

# OLIVE BRANCHES

You can do what you want
With the olive branches
That I've extended.
From where I'm standing
I can see the ashes.
As you burn the peace
That I offered to release,
The negative energy
Flowing through these streets.
If you hold on to anger,
And then say you're not mad,
Its like
drinking poison
And wishing I had.
You needed your gang
To oppose me.
Couldn't do it alone,
Just trying to expose me.
Insecurity set you on fire
Had to call in the troops;
Defended by liars.
Offended by my
Words? Then stop reading.
Your censorship suggestion
Was just you needing
To control me.
But you don't own me.
I don't live
To please you.
Here's a pacifier instead
To appease you.

# We Know

I could go on to explain and give detailed accounts of how badly his "episodes" ripped my heart up... but I don't need to; cause we know.

# The Climb

Making peace with
Past versions of yourself
Is not something you can do
In simple steps.
One at a time,
Its a tiring climb
So many things you'd
Rather just leave behind.
Not sure where the
Ladder even starts,
The rungs are rusty,
Tarnished from the blood
Of broken hearts.
The fear feels real but isn't
I think I need a minute
To compose myself and start again
Leave two decades of baggage
At the check-in.
They said my pain had purpose.
And I would rise above and
Turn it,
Into something that would heal me.
I agree, but it's not easy
To reprogram
everything you once knew,
Leave behind all the
Past versions of you.
Automatic behaviours
Need a rewrite.
Working on it,
Rome wasn't build in
One night.
But slow progress is better

Than none.
Look at all that
You've done.
Step one was to identify
That all of this time,
The enemy was
Operating on the front lines.

# The Fog

It's been foggy for weeks
And my mind feels it too.
Not sure if it's seasonal
or long-term
doom.

# DARK PLACES

The sadness is
Lifting
And I'm starting to breathe
Easily, it seems.
As if the weight of
Heavy ghosts
Is no longer
Pressing into me.
Anxiety loosening its grip.
For awhile, I was lost
And felt like
I was composed of
Shadows
And forests
And fog.
I had never been to
Those dark places
Before.
At least not for so long.

# Hot Tub Parties

Have you ever been in a hot tub
With two people who don't get along?
I have, and don't recommend it.
We used to have parties
In hot tubs
It was a New Year's Eve tradition
Liquor shots in ice glasses
That we could then
Conveniently smash onto
The side of the house.
It was around the time that The Arcade Fire got popular;
We thought it was cool that they were from our city
Gargoyles surrounding us
And several cats inside.
Tipsy and high
Dreading the inevitable step out on to fresh snow.
Mild flirtations happening right under his eyes
That went undetected for years.
How many boyfriends did you have to see,
In the hot tub, with me?
And you know, we never went into a hot tub
Together,
When I became your girlfriend.
But we did swim in a river, and
Got into a fight about two-doored vehicles
On the drive back from Boston.
That time I asked you to eat 5 cheeseburgers,
And you did, to make me laugh.

## Small Towns

And I guess that's what you get
when you live in a small town
and are a PISCES
and want to please everyone…

# Planes

When we're walking in the rain
And I ask you what you're afraid of
You say, planes.
And I find that so simple and heart-warming
Because, when you ask me
What I'm afraid of
I say, losing control and
Having a full-fledged panic attack
In a public place, like, for example
A grocery store, or an airport
Or even at a nice bakery
Or the library
And, of course,
After many years of reflection
I know this is, in essence
A fear of
Looking weak,
Or needing to ask for help
Or, not being in control
And can easily be fixed by,
Letting go of the need to
Control outcomes and just
Letting life happen and allowing
Planes to fly.

# Disappearing People

Sometimes it's weird
To think
Of the people
I have met and
Will probably never see again
So many people
Who fell through the cracks
Who showed up once
For supporting roles
Appearing briefly
And never coming back
Like co-workers
Bartenders
School mates
And first dates
Parents friends'
Will I ever
See them again?
And I know that ninety percent
Of the people that I meant
Are living in the country that I left
Which sort of answers the mystery
Of where they all went.

# Mom Brain

A total waste of mind,
To be thinking all the time
I had two babies, relax.
Stop trying to decode and define.
You just need to wait it out.
When they grow up, your mind
Will mellow out.
But right now, you can chill
Release the pressure and
Sit still.
You'll laugh at this one day,
When the fog has cleared away.
And you finally get some sleep,
Uninterrupted and deep.
With dreams and drool and
Messy hair.
And you sincerely won't even care.
That this period was sort of unfair.

## Ghosts Part II

your aura
needs a boost
or you've eaten too
many ghosts for
breakfast
or you just complain too
much about bitches
or you take things too
personally
or your ego is overactive,
and constantly offended
by the smallest of things
or maybe you just emit
an easy target vibe
after all,
he told me he could see
the shadow from the inside.
why do people see such darkness?
am I really that obvious?
but yeah, I kind of get it, too
maybe the blues
are literally seeping through.
and colouring in my once
bright and happy aura.
is there a product to
lighten this shit up
and get back
to normal?

# BROWN EYES

I like to think, Brown Eyes,
That somewhere in time,
We are walking over bridges,
And eating strawberries
Together, holding hands
Or Sitting up in bed,
Drinking beer out of
Coffee mugs, and feeling so
Much older than just 18.
I was dreading your trip to Europe,
Which would take you away,
As you counted the money,
That you had made,
At the dry cleaners, that day.
Counting down hours
Until we had to say,
Goodbye in the morning,
So quick and heartbreaking.
Just a couple of weeks
Where I stayed in your arms,
Safe from the world,
That was crumbling down.
And when you came back,
It was already done
And I never found out,
If you were the one.

Still, I didn't forget it
Even at 18, I meant it.
I missed what we
Could have been.
It was me who ruined
Everything.
So, I kept you alive
In my heart and my mind.
Imagining that,
You didn't leave me behind
After all of these years,
I still see you in dreams
Where we're free to be lovers
Without all the strings.

# Exhaustion

A complete mental and physical
Exhaustion, one that sort of
Reminds me of
The days where I drank
To escape the pain, and
The fear, back when I
Sprinkled everything
with wine and beer.
But now, things are alright
I have everything I need, and
The cycle of anxiety
Is just temporarily visiting me

# Elephant In The Room

Tears on the oversized T-shirt
That I took from your room.
Before you left, the second time,
When you stayed away for good.
And it broke my heart when I realized that
The distant
Look in your eyes
Was not going to disappear.
It had been there, already, for so many
Years.
Trying to avoid the
Elephant that lived in all the
Rooms
Of our beautiful home
Where we grew up happy, but not very strong.

# The Truth

I was a young dreamer,
Rummaging through the relics
Of your past.
Everything uncovered,
Was never going to last.
You left, and that meant
That we had to, too.
Counting the days, I had
Left in my room.
Where I grew up, and spent every
Night of my youth.
The first cut is the deepest
Now ain't that the truth.

# The Shimmer

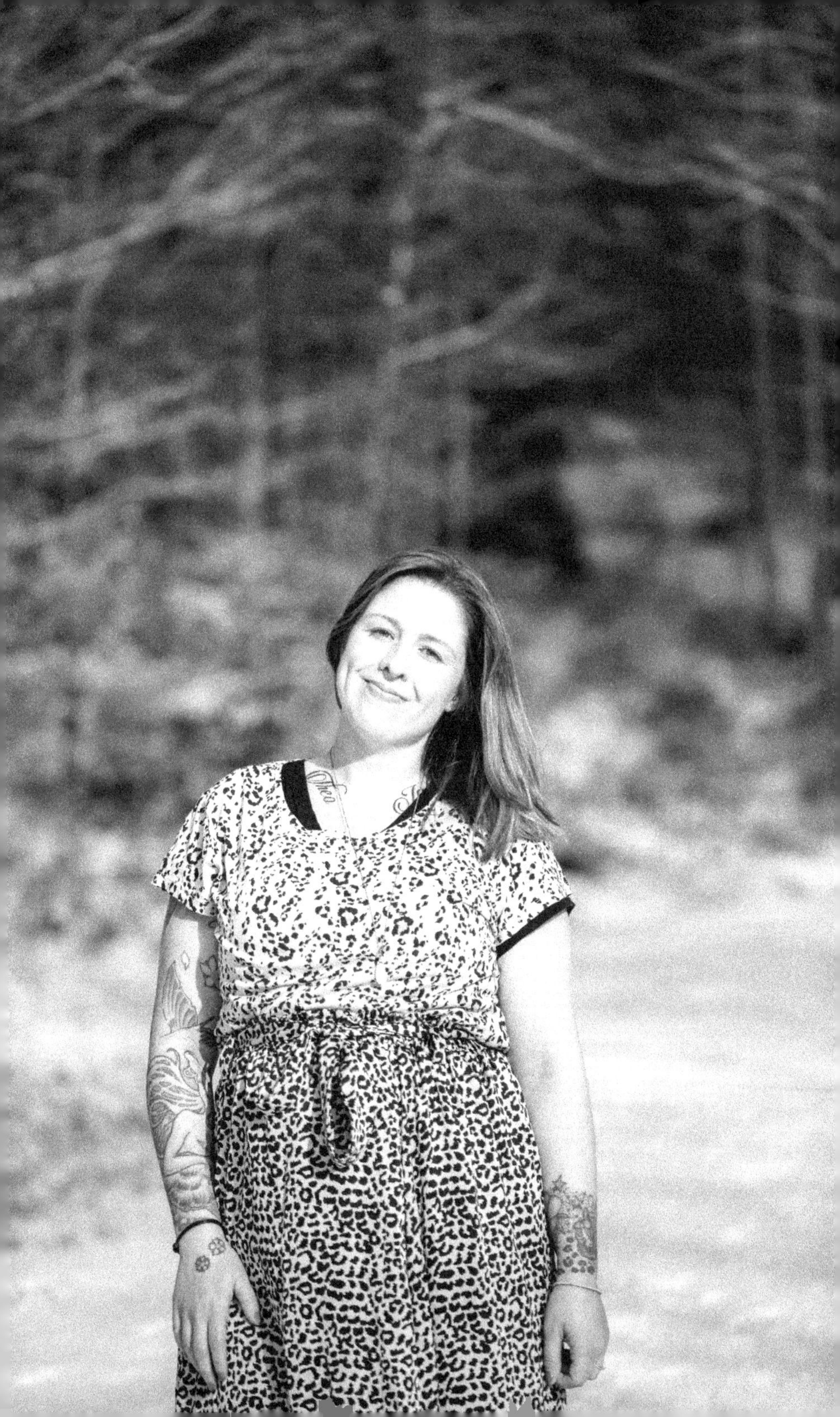

# Prud'homme

I had an oddly shaped
Bedroom, with a triangular
Corner closet
I slept above a
French bakery
While dreaming of a
Swiss chef
Everything was purple
These tones somehow calmed
Me
And I did my meditations, daily,
And waited for you to
Join me.

# On The Fence

I'm on the fence
But I'm on the side
That's alive
And this persistent fear
Needs to lay down
And die
A termination;
Living with ghosts
On the inside,
Its time.
Determination
The clouds came
Alive.
In my eyes,
I saw
Gold shining
Through;
Sourcing
From the inside.
The light was shadowed
Now it can't hide.
Stepping into
The brightness;
Leaving the forest
Behind.

# Miami Airport

The only flight we could
Get to Barbados
That time of year
Required a 9 hour layover
In the Miami Airport
And at first I thought,
This will be fun!
We can go to the beach and
Eat Cuban food and
Buy dolphin keychains
But security advised against
Leaving, due to long
Lines and wait times
So, with 9 hours to kill
we tried to vacation on
The inside

## Your Darkness

I fear the darkness
Inside of me
But you make dark things look so
Damn appealing;
I'm definitely healing.
You intrigue me.
Show me your drawings,
Let me interpret your feelings.

# Just Ariane

Sometimes it seems, I have
Searched for meaning
In my life, and felt that if
I somehow fit into a category
Or type of person, I would find
That I belonged
To a group, or to a
club, or some sort of secret
Society
Like, all of the people who
Like crystals, and full moons
And self-help books,
Please present yourselves.
Those who have babies born
Exactly eleven months and
twenty-two days apart,
Please stand up.
If you like pop music, but
Also like punk rock and
Sometimes country,
There is a club for that.
Those who have had issues
With anxiety, but also
Have a pretty good toolbox
For overcoming attacks,
You can sign in here.
If you want to stop drinking,
And smoking, you can follow
My Instagram page for that.
One day it occurred to me, that
I could still identify with all of
These subcategories,
Without virtually exhausting myself,

On the hunt for others
Who might be a little bit like me.
I am starting to realize, that
Being Just Ariane, is kind
Of fine.

# At First

I loved you at first for the simple things
Like how you had gentle eyes
And big hands that helped me unlace my dress
And we laughed when my dad showed up a little drunk
It was a wedding, after all
I could barely finish painting my toes the next day
When you arrived
I needed a steadier hand
In the garden I asked you to sit,
We were on to something.
Later, we held hands under a picnic table
Like little secret lovers who needed a fix
Stolen kisses behind a brick wall
We lay in the grass and looked up at the stars
More than one bottle of cheap champagne
Confessions and commitments
Through boozy breaths we swore
That destiny would join us
If it was written in the stars.

## June 15, 2015

Walk around until you feel no pain
Write until everything and nothing make sense anymore
Read to remember you're not the only one
Create to remember that you can

# Paris

Do you remember being with me,
In Paris?
We took a map and plotted our adventures
Each day a few different arrondissements
We walked everywhere,
And took the subway, just once
To get to a flea market in Clichy
Too bad, we didn't check the schedule
The market was empty, and you almost got
Robbed by a cross dresser
But later, you saved a man who took a sharp turn on his
Motorcycle, he shouldn't have put his large
Suitcase in his lap like that
I thought you were a hero, and walked around
Proud to hold your hand
One night we searched everywhere for a park
To have a picnic in
How on Earth did we not find one, it was Paris
After all
But it made us laugh, and we ended up making a
picnic on the steps
of the Academie Nationale de Musique
Which was a very romantic spot to sit
With buskers providing the entertainment
That week confirmed that it was you
That I could not live without
In Paris, and other cities, too

# Sheeps

They said I tried to turn you into
A teenage James Dean, and they weren't wrong
You probably knew that you were ridiculously good-looking,
but did an admirable job at staying modest
You even dated mere mortals, like me,
which proved that you weren't only concerned with looks
And I'm not saying that I was an ugly sixteen-year-old
Just that you were cute enough to date the extremely pretty girls
And, eventually you did.
We used to walk down to the French school
On the weekends, in the evening
And drink beer with purple slushes
I really thought I'd never let you go
Or that's how it felt in the moment
But, of course,
everyone thinks that when they're sixteen
and have a very handsome and
Romantic boyfriend, who was raised well
And had a lovely mother.
He wrote me love letters that I burnt when we broke up
I seem to have a bad habit of doing that.
But I do remember how he walked me home each night
Wrapped in his flannel shirts that smelled
Like fabric softener and cologne
We called each other Sheeps
Or Sheepie

And I spoke to him in a baby voice
Far too often
Another bad habit of mine, that I am glad to have
Finally overcome
And while we're on the subject of my high school love
Or at least one of them,
My Granny always said that he had immaculately white socks

# Tony Robbins

I'm super into Tony Robbins these days.
Am I the only one who has a little crush on
This massive man?
He's like 6'7 of pure happiness, joy
And motivation, wrapped into a horse.

# Tirupur

If you want to feel strong, you
Must remember the moments that you
Overcame obstacles, and challenges
When you didn't think that you could
For example, flying alone to India
Though you had aggressive
Panic attacks, at that time
And had just attended your sister's wedding
The night before, and had too many tequilas
And then had to pull up alongside a farm,
On the way to the airport, because you were sick
From the motion of the car and the anticipation
Of what would happen to you in India
But then, it was fine.
It was quite a spiritual experience.
Very crowded, which you don't like, but
These crowds were filled with people who didn't have
The affliction to overthink things, the way you Westerners do
So that naturally felt like a safer place to be
Among almost 1 million people,
Who live in the city of Tirupur, in the state of Tamil Nadu.
Which is the southern tip of India, very close to Sri Lanka
Where many of the world's cotton garments are made
And you were there to inspect pyjamas and
To learn a little bit more about clothing production
For 6 days, you ate bananas and granola bars
For fear of ingesting something contaminated
And getting ill, which would not have been ideal.
But you survived, and even came home with a
Beautiful selection of scarves and silver jewellery.
And a feeling of being stronger and more
spiritually awake, than you
Had been before.

## Scary Bits

When you stop running away from
What you think are the scary bits of life,
The scary bits lose their power

# Karen Jones' Daughter

Sometimes, when life is
Slightly challenging, I remember that
I am Karen Jones' Daughter
Which is comforting, because
Karen Jones is quite resilient to the
Pain and unfortunate circumstances
That life sometimes presents
And that makes me feel a little
Better; after all
I am her daughter, and must
Have some predisposition
To her spiritual strength
She has a twinkle in her eye that
Is very reassuring, because I know
Some of what she has overcome
And it is quite inspiring
And remarkable that, she hasn't
Hardened against
A world that is sometimes confusing
And that she still finds simple pleasures
In good books, and great finds
At markets, and bazaars and in local
Shops, where she always smiles
And makes people feel warm and
Fuzzy on the inside; it is a genuinely
Genuine kindness, what Karen Jones
Possesses, and I often think of what she told me
When I asked her how she
Never seemed to worry about
money, and the future
And she said, with a smile,
Well, I suppose it's because
I'm Reggie Jones' daughter

# Proposal

You proposed to me 5 days before we
Were going to get married
And I found that sweet, because
It wasn't a necessary proposal, but you
Know how much I love romantic
Gestures, and you made me
Spaghetti and told me to relax
It was on my mother's balcony
I knew you were up to something but I,
Just continued to drink cheap wine
And enjoy the fact that you would
Be my husband in 5 short days
While listening to country music
And feeling grateful that the 3
Stitches under my toe had healed well
You were on both knees and I made a
Joke that you should propose while
You were down there, which of course was
Your intention, all along

# Things That Shine

The magpie is a bird that is
Attracted to things that shine,
And my mother in law told me
That you must watch out around
Them, if you are wearing
Jewellery
Because, they can swoop down
And hurt you with their
Sharp beaks.
And I thought it was kind of sweet,
Because I would like to believe
That I am a thing that shines.
At least, under all the shadows,
On the inside.
And getting a beak straight in the
Heart would be a poetic
Way to go.
The magpie doesn't
Mean any harm.
Who can fault him for
Going after shiny things?
After all,
I tend to do the same.

## Switzerland, 2014

Sometimes, as I watch our babies play
And drink coffee that you made me
And wear a sweater that you bought me
I think about how crazy
And against all odds
Our story really is.
We met in a country that neither of us lived in
And then decided that it would be worthwhile,
To see if something could develop
Between us
Even though we lived 6,000 kilometers away from one another
And really didn't know much about each other
Except for what we disclosed in a rather drunken, tipsy tent

# Rooftops

I'm not usually relaxed
Enough to daydream
But today I found myself
Drifting off
And getting lost
In the pattern of the rooftops
Thinking about how
I love the symmetry
Of Swiss buildings
It was a nice pause
From the status quo
Doom and moss
And made for a much
More pleasant walk.

## No Surrender

For a nanosecond, I lost touch with my inner greatness
and my ability to
Stand on my own two feet; unassisted.
But that's not something I am surrendering.
Now, or ever.

# Baby Boy

I know you won't always need me
The way that you do now
With your warm hair against my cheek
And falling asleep
To the sound of a heartbeat,
That we once shared.
I know that you won't always need me
To kiss you softly, and sing you lullabies
Making sure that you know
That you have your own song.
I know that you won't always wake up
In the night, wondering, where I am
I'm right here, baby, it's alright.

# Paradox

The girl who theoretically believes that
The Universe is a safe and magical
Place, while battling panic disorder
The girl who longs to let go and
Rid the shackles that society has indoctrinated,
Yet, finds strange comfort in structure, rules
And symmetry.

# Labels

It's very liberating when you come to
realize, that you can stop putting yourself into
boxes, and categorizing
who you are, and what you've achieved
Little lists of accomplishments that we
carry around like badges
The truth is, for a long time
I did feel the need to say that I was great
Because I worked for a big fashion company
Or because I had half of a university degree
Or because I went to the gym a lot, at times
Or because, I never got fired from a job
Or let anyone break up with me first
But, it gets exhausting
To always lead with our roles

# Reinvent

It's strange to live in a country that you were
Not born in, but still feel at home, even though
Almost everyone you have ever known lives across
The ocean.
It's strange to go out and see people you know, but
Also know, that no one in this town has actually known you for
Longer than 5 years, and that includes your husband.
It's strange, but nice, to think that no one here
Knows anything about your high school haircuts
Or your former infatuation with boys
Or your past life as a booze-loving party girl.
You can reinvent yourself
In a new country,
When you have a new name
And have left everything you knew
Behind.

# On Immigrating To A New Country

Certainly, there have been
Blocks way bigger than this
In my past that I
Successfully kicked in the balls.

# Spas

I love going to spas with you
Because, they always seem to bring out
our silly sides, and we often get several
warnings, to whisper, and not disturb others
but we can't really help it, can we?
we don't get to speak so much, these days
unless it's over the noise of our babies
So the spas give us a chance
to remember a time when it was just you and me
telling each other secrets in the water; laughing
about the things that we did
together
when we were so much younger
and also,
before we knew each other

# Bajan Sun

We were, so much closer
To Venezuela and Guyana
Than we were to Switzerland
And Canada
With a sky that looked
Like it was entirely made up
Of pink cotton candy
Clouds
We went down to Oistens
And let the week continue
Drinking away the tension
That comes with big decisions
The moon was an upside
Down crescent
And I had never seen it like that
So close to the equator
That we could almost touch it

# Planets Near Pluto

Your energy was stronger than some
Of the new planets I photographed
Near Pluto
So, thank you
We all felt that.

## Little Particles

It's all pretty silly when you analyze things….
You break the fear down into little particles
until they turn into dust and
you realize they are illusions that don't even exist

# Falcon

I wanted to name you Falcon
And everyone laughed at me
Or looked at me funny
When I told them.
I was the only person who thought it
Was a really good name.
We could even spell it Falken,
The German way, like the
Dive bar in town
I guess I was just going through another one of my bird phases. You were born on Friday the 13$^{th}$
Proof that 13 isn't so unlucky
Right, baby Jake?

# Just A Mist

Perspective
Changes everything
From where I'm standing now
That fog is just a mist
And look how delicately it kisses
The mountains
The sun is shining
Blinding
Reminding
I hold the key
To my destiny
And my experience
Can be shadows, or be bliss
So what do you decide?
To be a dark thing
Or a thing that shines?

# Pink Clouds

Nothing makes me feel
Like things are going to
Be alright
Quite like the sight
Of pink clouds at night

# In The Valley

Cradled in the valley of
Dis-ease, with no peace
Just trying to find a
Way to keep my mind at ease
Something shifted,
And that valley is now
A bounty
Of love, my heart
Opened profoundly
I walk without fear;
Strong mountains beside me.

## Blood Moon Eclipse

There was a giant red moon
It was the longest
Eclipse of the century
And the stars aligned, perfectly;
I had my best friends next to me.
We held hands like children
And released what was no longer
Serving us
In the safety of each other's
Arms,
Moon beams shyly
Observing us

## Svetlana

You told me that
Gold was rare,
But you saw it in my eyes,
And on the insides.
We would speed walk to
The river
And share each others'
Secrets
You believed in magical things
Like the power of honey and butterfly wings.
And your eastern European sternness really proved to have a soft side.
Something golden, on the inside,
I recognized.

# 11 22

You know how much
I love numerology, and
Especially master numbers.
So, the fact that you
And your brother
Were born 11 months and
22 days apart,
Doesn't seem like a coincidence
To me.

# Never Retract

Stay brave, little ones
And don't let this hard,
Crumbling world
Dim the sparkle in your eyes.
Keep shining, from the inside.
Don't hide.
It'll be alright.
Momma's right here,
On your side.
Fighting to keep your
Hearts fully alive.
You know love doesn't
Die.
And it will get you
Through all the
Rough times.
Don't fall into the
Fear trap.
Momma knows a thing or
Two about that.
Just stay open, never retract.
This world is for you.
Let your heart be your
Road map.

# Three Sandwiches

Remember that time
My suitcase was accidentally
sent to Los Angeles?
And I had to wear leggings from the
Dollarama?
And you had made me
Three sandwiches, which were
Inside the suitcase.
They basically travelled
All around the world
In a matter of three days.

# The Words

For years, the words have
flowed through me;
thoughts scribbled frantically into notebooks,
perfectly constructed sentences
lulling me to sleep at the end of the day

# I Gave Up

I gave up alcohol before my problem got
too out of control;
before I lost too much of myself to the drink.
I gave up because I was horrified
at the prospect of being a drunk mom.
I gave up because I realized, during pregnancy,
that I was equally worthy of the love
and care that I had designated for my children.
I gave up because the person I wanted to be
could not mature while being fed
copious amounts of alcohol.
I gave up because I got bored of always being
drunk and moderately miserable.

# Sweet and Strong

There was a rose bush
On our front lawn
With hot pink petals
That smelled sweet and strong
In the summer the roses
Would bloom
And I
would turn those petals into
sweet perfume

# Freshly Cut Grass

On the subject of childhood
No, it wasn't all trauma
And daddy issues
And struggling within
My chubby body.
I have some wonderful
Memories.
Like waking up on a Saturday
And smelling freshly cut grass;
I can still hear the hum of
Our old lawn mower, if I close my eyes.
The sun shining into my
Bedroom window.
Warming a spot on my bed
Where my little dog, Wrinkles, would
Sleep, happily.
And I would get to work,
Organizing my bookshelf
In alphabetical order.
Preferably, with the books
In descending order
From tallest to shortest.

# Shining Beautifully

One of the earliest memories I have
Of being blissed out.
Swinging in the park.
Next to our house.
Feeling my spirits rising
with each push, felt like flying.
I would sing, like no one was watching.
And even if they were, I wasn't minding.
Back then, I had no fears, worries
Or troubles.
That's how I want to live again.
Step out of my bubble.
Break down the walls.
Let me free. I'm still inside here, shining
Beautifully.

# The Bright Side

They tried to scare me
But I'm fearless, now
They didn't realize that
My walls were built to
Break-down
A revolution,
On the inside
Nothing's forever,
That's the bright side

# Learning How To Be Alive

These streets
Don't seem as mean
As they used to be
The Shadows no longer clouding what I see.
Looking to the bright side,
Shining from the inside.
It took two decades
But I think I'm learning
How to be alive.

# A Final Thought

Moon magic, stuffing my bra with quartz and
Black tourmaline and sending blessings,
Love and heaps of understanding and
Forgiveness to all.